W9-ALN-813

BLACK HISTORY MAKERS

Athletes

Adam Sutherland

PowerKiDS
press™

New York

Published in 2012 by The Rosen Publishing Group, Inc.
29 East 21st Street, New York, NY 10010

Copyright © 2012 Wayland/The Rosen Publishing Group, Inc.

All rights reserved. No part of this book may be reproduced in any form without permission in writing from the publisher, except by a reviewer.

Editor: Katie Woolley, Jennifer Way
Designer: Tim Mayer, MayerMedia
Consultant: Mia Morris, Black History Month Web Site

Picture Acknowledgments: Cover, p. 17 Daniel Munoz/Reuters/Corbis; Title page, p. 12 Jerry Wachter/Sports Imagery/Getty Images; pp. 3, 21 Bob Thomas/Getty Images; p. 4 Eyre Crowe/Bridgeman Art Library/Getty Images; p. 5 Derek Cattani/Rex Features; p. 6 Fox Photos/Getty Images; p. 7 Keystone/Getty Images; p. 8 John Dominis/Time–Life Pictures/Getty Images; p. 9 Louise Gubb/CORBIS SABA/Corbis; p. 10 Lynn Goldsmith/Corbis; p. 11 Hulton Archive/Getty Images; p. 13 Michael Steele/Getty Images; pp. 14, 15, 16, 18, 19, 20 Shutterstock; p. 23 (bottom left) David Madison/New Sport/Corbis; p. 23 (bottom right) Clive Mason/AllSport/Getty Images; p. 23 (top right) PA/PA Archive/Press Association Images; p. 23 (bottom center) Stephen R. Schaefer/AFP/Getty Images; p. 23 (top center) Courtesy Geoff Thompson; p. 23 (top left) Ian Walton/Getty Images.

Library of Congress Cataloging-in-Publication Data

Sutherland, Adam.
Athletes / by Adam Sutherland. — 1st ed.
    p. cm. — (Black history makers)
Includes index.
ISBN 978-1-4488-6640-3 (library binding) — ISBN 978-1-4488-7058-5 (pbk.) — ISBN 978-1-4488-7059-2 (6-pack)
1. African American athletes—Biography. I. Title.
GV697.A1S847 2012
796.0922—dc23
[B]
                            2011029874

Manufactured in Malaysia

WEB SITES:

Due to the changing nature of Internet links, PowerKids Press has developed an online list of Web sites related to the subject of this book. This site is updated regularly. Please use this link to access the list:
www.powerkidslinks.com/blackhist/athletes/

CPSIA Compliance Information: Batch #WW2102PK: For Further Information contact Rosen Publishing, New York, New York at 1-800-237-9932

CONTENTS

Making History

From the early 1600s to the 1800s, slaves were brought from Africa and sold in slave markets in the Americas. This slave trade brought more than four million African slaves to work on large **plantations** in the American south. The Civil War (1861–1865) was fought to end slavery in the United States, but even after it was **abolished** in 1865, **segregation** and **racial prejudice** remained.

Fighting Prejudice

Black athletes have had to overcome hardships and obstacles, and achieving success has not always been easy. The athletes featured in this book have had to fight **economic** and social segregation and **racism** to reach the top of their chosen sport.

These slaves are being sold at a slave market.

Olympic Success and Failure

The struggles of black people continued into the twentieth century. By the 1930s, successful black athletes were rare and a black Olympic champion like Jesse Owens (page 6) was one in a million. Owens's four gold medals at the 1936 Berlin Olympics were all the more important because he was competing against Adolf Hitler's plans to produce a white German "super race." Owens may have been an Olympic champion, but he continued to face racial problems back in the United States.

Black Power

The late 1960s and early 1970s was the era of **black power** in the United States. This was the embracing of black pride and identity and the advancement of black values by a generation of African Americans.

Although not formally associated with the black power movement, heavyweight boxer Muhammad Ali (page 10) showed the world what it meant to be black and proud. Ali's intelligence and showmanship, as well as his abilities in the ring and his refusal to fight for a "white" U.S. Army in the unpopular Vietnam War, made him a perfect role model for the cause.

Continued Racial Discrimination

Some sports became racially **desegregated** more quickly than others. The first African American to sign a National Basketball Association (NBA) contract was Nat Clifton in 1950. In golf, however, the Augusta National Golf Club in Georgia which hosts the sport's Major Championships every year, did not accept black members until 1990.

Looking to the Future

It is now nearly 100 years since Jesse Owens, the first history maker profiled in this book, was born. A lot of changes have taken place since then and black athletes around the world can finally stand shoulder to shoulder with their white competitors.

Sprinters Tommie Smith (center) and John Carlos (right) gave the black power movement's famous "black power salute" at the 1968 Summer Olymipics.

Jesse Owens
Record-Setting Runner

James Cleveland Owens was the seventh of eleven children. At nine, a schoolteacher misheard his initials "J.C." as "Jesse" and the nickname stuck. Owens developed his passion for running thanks to the support and encouragement of his school coach, Charles Riley. Jesse's family were poor, so he delivered groceries and worked in a shoe repair shop to help put food on the table.

Name: James Cleveland "Jesse" Owens

Born: September 12, 1913, Oakville, Alabama

Died: March 31, 1980

Sport: Track and field

Awards and titles: Four gold medals at the 1936 Summer Olympics, world records in the long jump, 220-yard sprint and 220-yard hurdles

Interesting fact: Has an asteroid named after him, 6758 Jesseowens.

Owens enjoyed success in the 1936 Olympic Games in Berlin, Germany, but was unable to compete as an **amateur** athelete afterward.

Highs and Lows

In 1933, while at high school in Cleveland, Ohio, Owens equaled the world record of 9.4 seconds in the 100-yard dash. Owens was wanted by many college track teams. Ohio State University helped his father find a job so Owens could study and train there. In 1935, Owens set three world records and equaled a fourth all in one day! These successes did not change his social status, however. Because of racial segregation, the legal separation of whites and African Americans, Owens had to live off-campus with other black athletes. When he traveled with the team he ate in "black-only" restaurants and slept in "black-only" hotels.

> **"** I wasn't invited to shake hands with Hitler, [but] I wasn't invited to the White House to shake hands with the president, either. **"**
>
> *Jesse Owens*

Jesse Owens's four gold medals at the 1936 Olympics put him in the history books.

Olympic Gold

The Berlin Olympics in 1936 made Owens a legend. He won gold medals in the 100-meter sprint, long jump, 200-meter sprint and 4 x 100 meters relay. As an amateur athlete, Owens received no prize money for his wins. So, when he was offered "appearance money" to compete in specially organized events after the Olympics, Owens accepted it. A poor man all his life, the temptation to earn some money for his family was too great.

Until recently, the Olympics were only open to unpaid amateur athletes. Being paid to race made Owens a professional in the eyes of officials, and they withdrew Owens's amateur status. Unable to compete again against the world's best, Owens traveled widely, making speeches to youth groups and corporate organizations. He continued to inspire people until his death in 1980.

MAKING HISTORY

Just before the 1936 Games, Owens was visited at the Olympic Village by Adi Dassler, the founder of Adidas, who persuaded Owens to run in Adidas shoes. It was the first sponsorship of a male African American athlete in history.

Kipchoge Keino
The Inspirational Runner

- Name: Kipchoge "Kip" Keino
- Born: January 17, 1940, Kipsamo, Nandi District, Kenya
- Sport: Track and field
- Awards and titles: Gold medals at the 1968 and 1972 Olympics and Chairman of the Kenyan Olympic Committee since 1999
- Interesting fact: In the Nandi language Kipchoge means "born near the grain storage shed."

Keino won a gold medal at the 1972 Olympics in the 3,000 meter steeplechase.

Early Life

Kip Keino was born into a group of the Kalenjin tribe called the Nandi, in Kenya. As a child, Keino herded goats on Kenya's hilly countryside and used his spare time to practice running. His father, a long-distance runner himself, encouraged his son in the sport. This was **high-altitude** training, meaning that the oxygen content in the air was lower in the steep, hilly area in which Keino ran. This training helped Keino develop great **stamina**.

Fighting Spirit

After both his parents died, Keino was brought up by an aunt. When he left school, Keino joined the Kenyan police. He continued to run in his spare time, and in 1965, he broke onto the world stage, setting two world records in the 3,000 meters and 5,000 meters races.

By 1965, he was traveling around the world to race. At the 1966 Commonwealth Games he won gold in the one-mile and three-mile races.

Olympic Glory

Keino arrived at the 1968 Summer Olympics in Mexico City with stomach pains that were later diagnosed as a severe bladder infection. On the day of the 1,500 meters final, doctors told Keino he was still too ill to race, but he decided that he owed it to his country to at least compete. Keino was caught in traffic on the way to the stadium. He got out of the car and ran the last mile to the stadium, before completing the race in first place in an Olympic record time! Keino also won a silver medal in the 5,000-meters race. He ran for Kenya again in the 1972 Summer Olympics in Munich, Germany. There he won a gold medal for the 3,000-meters steeplechase and a silver medal in the 1,500-meters race.

Helping Children

After retiring from the sport in 1975, Keino and his wife Phyllis set up an orphanage, the Kip Keino Children's Home. The project has now grown to include the Kip Keino School, teaching almost 300 children from ages 6 to 13. Keino is also Chairman of the Kenyan Olympic Committee. In 1996, he joined the World Sports **Humanitarian** Hall of Fame.

Keino has devoted his life to helping those less fortunate than himself in his home country. Here, he is jogging across the Kenyan countryside with orphans in 1996.

MAKING HISTORY

Kip Keino's Olympic success inspired the country's dominance of long distance running. Since 1968, Kenya has won every 3,000-meter Olympic steeplechase it has entered. Kenya continues to struggle with poverty, but on the track, thanks to Keino, it has a source of hope and pride.

Muhammad Ali
The Greatest

Muhammad Ali was born Cassius Clay in rural Kentucky. Clay started boxing under local trainer Fred Stoner. Fast and strong, he excelled at the sport and blazed a trail through the amateur ranks, winning six Kentucky Golden Gloves, two national Golden Gloves, and a Light Heavyweight gold medal at the 1960 Summer Olympics in Rome, Italy. After his Olympic triumph, Clay turned professional and progressed steadily through the ranks, winning his first 19 professional fights. This success earned him the right to fight World Champion Sonny Liston, whom he defeated, in February 1964.

Name: Cassius Marcellus Clay Jr. (changed his name to Muhammad Ali in 1964)

Born: January 17, 1942, Louisville, Kentucky

Sport: Boxing

Awards and titles: Olympic gold medal, three World Heavyweight titles

Interesting fact: One of Ali's fights inspired Sylvester Stallone to write the original *Rocky* film.

Muhammad Ali was a world star both in and out of the boxing ring.

Religious Beliefs

After defeating Liston, Clay announced that he had converted to Islam and had been given the name Muhammad Ali. He continued boxing and successfully defended his title several times.

In 1967, Ali was called up to fight for the U.S. Army in the Vietnam War, but he refused to serve. Ali was stripped of his heavyweight title and his boxing license and did not fight again for three years. He made a living speaking at antiwar gatherings at colleges and universities around the country.

> " Hating people because of their color is wrong... It doesn't matter which color does the hating. It's just plain wrong. "
>
> *Muhammad Ali*

Muhammad Ali (then Cassius Clay) won his first world title in 1964, beating Sonny Liston.

Big Fights

In 1970, Ali was granted a new license and stepped back into the ring. The final stage of his career was by far the most memorable. He fought and defeated fellow heavyweight champions Joe Frazier and George Foreman in some of the best-remembered boxing matches of all time.

In a professional career that spanned from 1960 to 1981, Ali won 56 fights and lost only five. After retiring from the sport, he was diagnosed with **Parkinson's disease**. Despite the illness, Ali remains an active public figure today. He has been on Middle Eastern peace missions with the United Nations and been presented with peace medals for his humanitarian efforts.

MAKING HISTORY

Muhammad Ali was the best known black athlete of his day. His intelligence and achievements gave young African Americans a role model to identify with. As a prominent black Muslim, he also helped to raise understanding of his religion and beliefs.

Michael Jordan
Basketball Superhero

Michael Jordan grew up in Wilmington, North Carolina, and attended the University of North Carolina, where he excelled at basketball. He was named Player of the Year and scored the winning basket in the 1982 NCAA championships.

Name: Michael Jeffrey Jordan

Born: February 17, 1963, Brooklyn, New York

Sport: Basketball

Awards and titles: Six NBA Championships with the Chicago Bulls and voted greatest North American athlete of the 20th century by ESPN

Interesting fact: Jordan had a sneaker made in his honor, the Nike Air Jordan.

Here is Jordan competing against Washington for the Chicago Bulls in 1991.

Success in the NBA

He joined the Chicago Bulls in 1984 and quickly emerged as the best player the NBA had ever seen. His jumping abilities earned him the nickname "Air Jordan." With Jordan in the team, the Bulls won six NBA titles and Jordan himself was named the league's Most Valuable Player five times.

Making History

In 2000, Michael Jordan was named ESPN Athlete of the Century. His popularity brought new fans and advertisers to the sport and the current generation of NBA stars credit him as their inspiration for taking up the sport.

> " I realize that I'm black, but I like to be viewed as a person and this is everybody's wish. "

Kelly Holmes
The Golden Girl

Kelly Holmes won gold medals in the 800 meters and the 1,500 meters at the 2004 Olympics in Athens, Greece.

Name: Dame Kelly Holmes MBE, DBE

Born: April 19, 1970, Pembury, Kent, United Kingdom

Sport: Middle-distance running

Awards and titles: Two Olympic gold medals, British record holder at 600 meters, 800 meters, 1,000 meters, and 1,500 meters

Interesting fact: Holmes was a British Army judo champion.

Kelly Holmes started running at 12 years old and won the English schools 1,500 meters title the following year. However, she left athletics at 18 to join the British Army. At first she drove trucks before retraining as a physical training instructor and rose to the rank of sergeant.

Back to Athletics

Holmes returned to the track in 1992, and she won a bronze medal in the 2000 Summer Olympics in Sydney, Australia. Holmes won gold medals in the 800 meters and 1,500 meters in the 2004 Summer Olympics in Athens, Greece. She retired in 2005 and is currently fronting the government's School Olympics initiative to get competitive sport back into the playground.

MAKING HISTORY

In 2009, Kelly Holmes established the DKH Legacy Trust, which encourages young people to take part and excel in sports and helps disadvantaged young people to find and believe in their own talents. Holmes also played an important role in London's winning bid to host the 2012 Summer Olympic Games.

Tiger Woods
Golfing Phenomenon

Name: Eldrick Tont "Tiger" Woods

Born: December 30, 1975, Cypress, California

Sport: Golf

Awards and titles: 14 Major Championships, Professional Golf Association (PGA) Player of the Year a record 10 times

Interesting fact: Tiger was raised as a Buddhist and practiced the faith from childhood well into his twenties.

Tiger Woods is the most successful golfer of modern times, having won 14 Major Championships.

Childhood Talent

Tiger Woods was introduced to golf at two years old by his father, Earl. By the age of three he was playing on adult golf courses, at five he was appearing on national television. Before the age of seven, he had already won an Under Age 10 golf tournament and at eight he won the first of six Junior World Golf Championships. He was also the first golfer to win the U.S. Junior Amateur title three years in a row.

Going Professional

In 1994, Woods earned a golf scholarship to the prestigious Stanford University in California. He left after two years to become a professional golfer. Professional golf is historically a white sport. One of the most famous courses, Augusta National in Georgia, only began accepting African American members in 1990. Fortunately, Tiger Woods's talent helped to turn this prejudice on its head.

> **"** Growing up, I came up with this name: I'm a "Cablinasian." As in Caucasian-black-Indian"Asian. I'm just who I am. **"**
>
> *Tiger Woods*

The Majors

There are four Major Championship golf tournaments every year. They are the U.S. Masters Tournament, the PGA, the British Open Championship, and the U.S. Open Championship. Nine months after turning professional, Woods won his first Major at the U.S. Masters Tournament with a record score, becoming the youngest-ever winner and the first African American to win.

Hot Property

Tiger Woods has single-handedly expanded golf's popularity. His amazing golfing success and broad public appeal have made him one of the world's most recognizable athletes. Woods continues to compete and hopes to one day match veteran player Jack Nicklaus's 18 Major Championship victories.

Here is Tiger Woods playing in Bangkok, Thailand, in November 2010.

Venus and Serena Williams
Record-Breaking Sisters

Venus and Serena Williams starting playing tennis at four and five years old, respectively. It was their father Richard's dream that one day both girls would become professional tennis players. At the time, the family lived in the dangerous Compton area of Los Angeles, and the sisters practiced on damaged public courts.

Names: Venus Ebony Starr Williams, Serena Jameka Williams

Born: Venus: June 17, 1980, Lynwood, California

Serena: September 26, 1981, Saginaw, Michigan

Sport: Tennis

Awards and titles: Venus: 7 Grand Slam singles titles, 12 doubles titles. Serena: 13 Grand Slam singles titles, 12 doubles titles

Interesting fact: Venus has a faster average serve than Roger Federer and Rafael Nadal.

Venus (left) and Serena are known for their colorful tennis outfits and eye-catching hairstyles on the court.

Tennis Childhood

Richard and his then-wife Oracene (now Oracene Price) were so eager for Venus and Serena to pursue tennis careers that they moved the family to Florida to enroll the girls at a tennis academy. However, their parents did not agree with the academy's methods and decided to coach the girls themselves so they could focus on their schoolwork while they grew as tennis players. Richard even gave up his job to coach them full-time. The hard work paid off. At age 17, Venus reached the final of the U.S. Open in her first attempt. Two years later, Serena, then 17, won it.

66 You have to believe in yourself when no one else does. That makes you a winner right there. 99

Venus Williams

Super Skills

Both sisters are tall and very strong, with powerful serves (Venus has the fastest serve in women's tennis. Serena has the second fastest.), great forehands and backhands, good volleys, and accurate baseline games. Between them, Venus and Serena are first and second all-time money winners in female sports with around $30 million each.

Serena (left) and Venus are hard to beat in a doubles championship. Here they are competing and winning a match in the 2009 Australian Open Doubles Championship.

Helping Hands

Both sisters are also committed to charity work. Serena helped fund the Serena Williams Secondary School in Kenya and has supported programs focusing on at risk young people. Venus works alongside her mother helping The Owl Foundation, which supports children with learning disabilities.

MAKING HISTORY

In tennis, the world's best players measure themselves against success in four Grand Slams. They are the Australian Open, the French Open, the U.S. Open, and Wimbledon. Between them, Venus and Serena Williams have won 20 Grand Slam singles titles and competed together to win 12 doubles titles.

❝ If you can keep playing tennis when somebody is shooting a gun down the street, that's concentration. ❞
Serena Williams

Lewis Hamilton
Formula One Star

If one man was born for speed, it is Lewis Hamilton. Named after gold-medal winning American sprinter Carl Lewis, he started racing go-karts at eight years old and a year later finished second in the national adult championships. Hamilton's father, Anthony, always supported his son. He left his job as an IT manager and sometimes worked three part-time jobs to have the flexibility to attend all of Hamilton's races.

Name: Lewis Carl Davidson Hamilton, MBE

Born: January 7, 1985, Stevenage, Hertfordshire, United Kingdom

Sport: Formula One racing

Awards and titles: Formula One World Champion 2008

Interesting fact: He is the youngest championship leader, and the only driver since the series started in 1950 to finish all of his first seven races on the podium.

Lewis Hamilton burst onto the Formula One scene with a record-breaking four race wins in his debut season.

Young Dreams

At ten years old, Hamilton met the McLaren Formula One team boss Ron Dennis and told him, "One day I want to be racing your cars..." Dennis wrote in Hamilton's autograph book, "Call me in nine years, we'll sort something out." In 1998, Dennis signed Hamilton to the McLaren driver development program.

World Champion

With his combination of lightning-fast reflexes and a burning desire to succeed, Hamilton excelled at all levels of motor racing. He has been a winner at every stage of his driving career, from British Formula Renault (where he was U.K. series champion in 2003) and Formula Three Euroseries (where he was Drivers' Champion in 2005) to Formula One, where he finished second in his first season, in 2007. He became the sport's youngest World Champion in 2008. One hundred percent professional, hard-working, and dedicated to his sport, Hamilton is destined for many more years of success.

Hamilton makes a high-speed turn during the 2009 Malaysian Grand Prix.

> "Being black is not a negative. It's a positive... because I'm different... It can open doors to different cultures and that is what motor sport is trying to do."

Lewis Hamilton

MAKING HISTORY

Black role models in motor racing were nonexistent until Lewis Hamilton, son of a white mother and black father, set his sights on Formula One success. The first black driver in Formula One, Hamilton has opened up an historically white sport to a wider audience, inspiring young people everywhere to follow in his footsteps.

Usain Bolt
Lightning Bolt

Here is Usain Bolt celebrating after setting a new world record in the 100 meters in 2008.

Name: Usain St. Leo Bolt

Born: August 21, 1986, Trelawny, Jamaica

Sport: Track and field

Awards and titles: Three Olympic gold medals (2008), five World Championship gold medals (2009), world and Olympic record-holder

Interesting fact: Usain won the 2008 Olympic gold medal for the 100 meters Olympic gold medal with one shoelace undone.

Humble Beginnings

Usain Bolt grew up in a small town in Jamaica, where his parents ran the local grocery store. Soccer and cricket were his favorite sports, but a local coach encouraged his sprinting abilities. By the age of 12, Bolt was the fastest runner at his school. He won his first high school championship medal in 2001, earning a silver in the 200 meters and a time of 22.04 seconds. He then competed in the 2002 World Junior Championships in Kingston, Jamaica. He won the 200 meters and at 15 years old, he became the youngest-ever world junior gold medallist.

Olympic Success

A leg injury hurt his performance in the 2004 Summer Olympics. He set the world on fire at the 2008 Summer Olympics in Beijing, China, though. Bolt won the 100 meters in a world record-setting 9.69 seconds. This achievement was made even more remarkable because he visibly slowed before the line to celebrate his victory!

He then set both world and Olympic records of 19.30 seconds in the 200 meters. Two days later, he was part of the gold medal-winning 4 x 100 meters relay team. This team also broke world and Olympic records. Bolt was the first sprinter to win two gold medals since American Carl Lewis in 1984.

Usain Bolt won the gold medal in the 100 meters at the 2008 Olympics in Beijing, China.

World Championships

At the 2009 World Championships in Berlin, Germany, Bolt repeated his success with gold medals in the 100 meters, 200 meters and 4 x 100 meters relay. In the 100 meters and 200 meters, Bolt beat his own world records with times of 9.58 seconds and 19.19 seconds, respectively. Usain Bolt is one of the fastest runners in the world.

MAKING HISTORY

With a population of just 2.8 million, Jamaica has had an amazing tradition of Olympic sprinting success since they first entered the Olympics in 1948. Usain Bolt is following in the footsteps of fellow Jamaican medal winners Arthur Wint, Don Quarrie, and Merlene Ottey. His record-breaking runs are inspiring young Jamaicans to take up track and field, rather than other sports. Bolt's success ensures that a new crop of Jamaican runners will compete on the world stage for years to come.

More Sports Heroes

Sir Garfield St. Aubrun Sobers (1936–)

This former West Indies cricket team captain is known as one of the sport's greatest-ever players. Born in Bridgetown, Barbados, Sobers played for the West Indies team for 20 years, from 1954 to 1974. He set numerous records for his achievements. He was knighted in 1975 for his services to the sport of cricket.

Edison Arantes do Nascimento "Pelé" (1940–)

Pelé was born in Três Corações, Brazil, and is the all-time leading goal scorer of the Brazilian national soccer team. Fast, powerful and able to shoot with either foot, he scored 1,283 goals in a career that lasted from 1956 to 1977. He is the only player to be part of three World Cup-winning teams (1958, 1962, 1970).

Tessa Sanderson (1956–)

This gold medal-winning javelin thrower was born in Jamaica but emigrated to England and competed for the United Kingdom. She appeared in a record six Olympic Games and was the first black woman to win an Olympic gold medal in 1984.

Geoff Thompson (1958–)

Thompson was a five time WUKO World Karate Champion from 1982 to 1986 and the highest competitive point scorer in the history of the sport. For the past 15 years, Thompson has led the Youth Charter, a charity that fights gang culture and promotes the positive effects of sports on kids and teens around the world.

Dikembe Mutombo (1966–)

Mutombo is a retired Congolese-American basketball player. He played for teams including the New York Knicks (2003–2004) and the Houston Rockets (2004–2009). He has donated millions of dollars to improve living conditions in the Democratic Republic of the Congo and is a Youth Emissary for the United Nations.

Marlon Shirley (1978–)

Shirley is the first parathelete to break 11 seconds in the 100 meters. He was abandoned by his mother and lived in orphanages. He lost his leg at the age of five in an accident, but sports helped Shirley get his life back on track. He won gold in the 100 meters in both the 2000 and 2004 Paralympics.

Timeline

Legacy

1936 Jesse Owens wins four Olympic gold medals in Berlin

1964 Cassius Clay beats Sonny Liston to become World Heavyweight Champion

1968 Kip Keino wins an Olympic gold medal in the 1,500 meters in Mexico City

1970 Pelé captains Brazil to a World Cup victory against Italy

1974 Muhammad Ali beats George Foreman to regain his World Heavyweight title

1982 Geoff Thompson wins the first of five consecutive WUKO World Karate Championships

1984 Tessa Sanderson is the first black woman to win an Olympic Gold medal

1991 Michael Jordan wins the first of six NBA Championships

1995 Dikembe Mutombo wins NBA Defensive Player of the Year award

1997 Tiger Woods wins his first U.S. Masters Tournament

1999 Serena Williams wins the U.S. Open

2000 Venus Williams wins Wimbledon

2000 Marlon Shirley wins the gold in the 100 meters at the Sydney Paralympics

2004 Kelly Holmes wins gold medals in the 800 meters and 1,500 meters at the Athens Olympics

2004 Marlon Shirley wins the gold in the 100 meters, silver in the 200 meters and bronze in the long jump at the Athens Paralympics

2008 Usain Bolt wins three gold medals at the Beijing Olympics

2008 Lewis Hamilton becomes a Formula One World Champion

2009 Usain Bolt wins three Gold medals at the World Championships

2010 Serena Williams wins Wimbledon

The legacies of the atletes in this book live on, not only in their achievements but also through the charities they and their families have founded:

The Tiger Woods Foundation: http://web.tigerwoodsfoundation.org/index
Established by Tiger and his father Earl. The charity focuses on projects for children, from golf clinics to university scholarships.

The Muhammad Ali Center: http://www.alicenter.org/Pages/default.aspx
Its message, according to Ali, is "peace, social responsibility, respect and personal growth."

The Serena Williams Foundation: http://theswf.org/
Set up to provide education and support for children from underprivileged backgrounds, and those affected by violent crime.

The DKH Legacy Trust: http://www.dkhlegacytrust.org/
The charity's team of Olympians, Paralympians, World, Commonwealth, and European Champions work with children to "create chances for young people."

Glossary

abolish (uh-BAH-lish) To put an end to something, for example abolish slavery.

amateur (A-muh-chur) A sportsman or woman who does not get paid to compete in their chosen sport.

black power (BLAK POW-er) A movement in 1960s America that united black people by emphasising pride in their race's achievements.

desegregated (dee-SEH-gruh-gayt-id) An end to racial separation.

economic (eh-kuh-NAH-mik) A term relating to the finances of a country or an individual.

high-altitude (HY AL-tuh-tood) An area that is high above sea level.

humanitarian (hyoo-man-ih-TAYR-ee-un) A person who wants to help to improve the welfare and happiness of others.

parathlete (per-ATH-leet) An athlete who has a handicap and who takes part in contests with athletes with similar handicaps

Parkinson's disease (PAR-kin-sinz dih-ZEEZ) A disease believed to be caused by the deterioration of a person's brain cells. Sufferers often experience trembling of the fingers and hands and slow speech.

plantation (plan-TAY-shun) A large estate or farm where crops are grown and tended to by workers.

racial prejudice (RAY-shul PREH-juh-dis) The belief that people from different races do not deserve the same rights, freedoms or respect as your own race.

racism (RAY-sih-zum) Hatred or intolerance of another race or races.

segregation (seh-grih-GAY-shun) The separation of people of different races by a country's government.

stamina (STA-mih-nuh) A person's strength or ability to resist tiredness.

Index